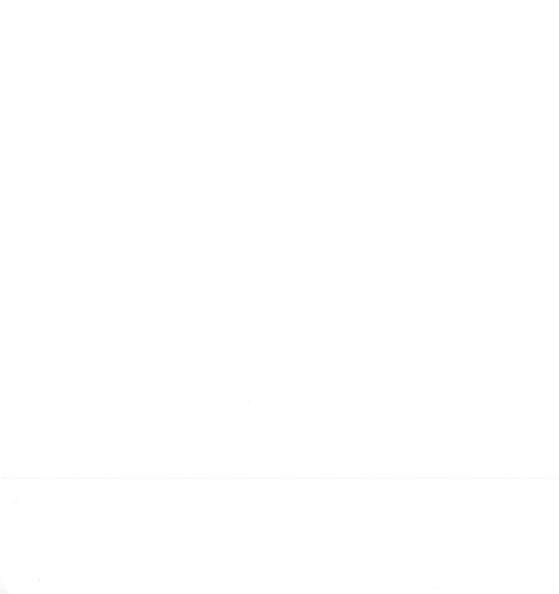

OUR SUPER ADVENTURE

A DIARY COMIC BY SARAH GRALEY

♡ Sarah Graley

ISBN: 9780993384325

OUR SUPER ADVENTURE

COPYRIGHT 2016 SARAH GRALEY
ALL RIGHTS RESERVED

SECOND PRESSING

PUBLISHED BY SHINY SWORD PRESS,
BIRMINGHAM, UK

FOR STEF.

THEME PARKIN'

SARAH!

WEH?

OH MY GOD

PLUSH DOUGHNUT PRIZES!!

SPIN WHEEL

SOON

I SPENT ALL MY MONEY WINNING THIS

THIS IS WHAT BEING AN ADULT IS...

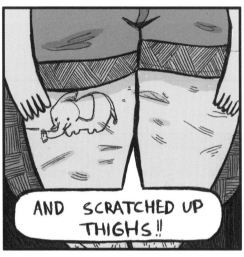

9

13

19

YOU'RE READING THOSE COMIC PAGES TOO FAST.

YOU GOTTA TAKE TIME TO DRINK THAT ARTWORK IN.

SLURP SLURP SLURP

KIDS AT SCHOOL KEEP ASKING FOR MY GAMER ID.

IT'S A SILLY ID

YOUR USERNAME ON EVERYTHING IS 'IMDRACULA' AND YOU CAN'T EVEN NAME 3 DRACULA MOVIES!!

YES I CAN!! THERE'S DRACULA, NOSFERATU,

AND THE BEST OF THEM ALL, DRACULA 2: ELECTRIC BOOGALOO.

37

MY FACE HAS BEEN PINK CONSISTANTLY FOR THE PAST HALF HOUR

I THINK IT'S THE WINE. I NEVER DRINK WINE.

YOU COULD... STOP DRINKING IT...?

BUT IT'S FREEEEE!!

45

SLEEPING IN THE SAME ROOM AS FRIENDS

GOOD MORNING!!

EY

DID I FART IN MY SLEEP?

YOU'RE LOOKING AT WILSON LIKE YOU'RE GONNA EAT HIM.

WHAT!!! THIS IS MY I LOVE YOU LOOK!

IT'S THE SAME LOOK YOU HAVE FOR HAMBURGERS.

SMOOCH
SMOOCH
SMOOCH!!

63

LOOK AT ALL THE JELLY I MADE!

YOU KNOW EVERYONE COMING OVER LATER IS VEGAN, RIGHT?

SO?

IT'S ALL FOR ME!

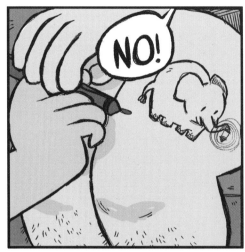

97

I WAS TALKING TO MY DAD ABOUT LASER EYE SURGERY.

THEY ADVERTISE IT PER EYE.

MAYBE I SHOULD GET ONE DONE AND GET A PRESCRIPTION MONOCLE!

THAT IS SO STUPID

HEY, THATS EXACTLY WHAT MY DAD SAID!

107

115

EARLIER

COOL

buzz buzz buzz

I NEED TO WASH MY TATTOO, BUT I'M SCARED OF MESSING IT UP...

YOU'LL BE FINE.

THE COLOURS RUNNING! IT'S ALL GOOPY!

MY TATTOO'S MELTING OFF!

SARAH—

AAAH!!!

I HAVE A CAT IN EACH ARMPIT!

PURR

139

149

HERE'S A PICTURE OF STEF AND ONE OF OUR CATS!

AW, CUTE.

I MISS HIM...

STEF?

NO, THE CAT.

189

✦ OLD STRIPS REDRAWN

✦ T-SHIRT CORNER

✦ OUR CATS

✧ T-SHIRT CORNER ✧

JOHNNY FOREIGNER I.

TELLISON

EXPENSIVE

JOHNNY FOREIGNER II.

TYRANNOSAURUS DEAD

ZELDA

LOS CAMPESINOS

ADVENTURE TIME

SOMEONE STILL LOVES
YOU, BORIS YELTSIN

TRUSTFUND

ONSIND

DAD ROCKS

SCREAMING MALDINI

JOHNNY FOREIGNER III.

ALKALINE TRIO

JOHNNY FOREIGNER IV.

LIGHTNINGHEART RECORDS

SONIC THE COMIC

✧✧ THE SUPER ADVENTURERS ✧✧

SARAH GRALEY WAS BORN IN NORTHAMPTON, UK, AND NOW LIVES IN
BIRMINGHAM WITH STEF, AND THEIR MANY, MANY CATS.
SHE HAS BEEN DRAWING OUR SUPER ADVENTURE SINCE 2012,
ALONGSIDE OTHER COMICS ABOUT QUESTS AND PIZZA THAT
YOU CAN FIND AT WWW.SARAHGRALEY.COM

STEF WAS BORN ON THE MOON, SPACE.
HE MAKES VIDEOGAME MUSIC AT TINYSPELLS.BANDCAMP.COM,
AND BASICALLY DOES EVERYTHING IN 'SONIC THE COMIC',
THE BAND HIM AND SARAH PLAY POP SONGS IN.

✨ OUR CATS ✨ (THE REAL STARS OF OUR SUPER ADVENTURE)

SPECIAL THANKS TO MY PARENTS, WHO
HAVE ALWAYS SUPPORTED AND ENCOURAGED
MY ART.
THANKS TO STEF, FOR NOT ONLY IS HE THE
CUTEST HUMAN THAT LETS ME DRAW COMICS
ABOUT HIM, BUT HE ALSO HELPED ME PUT
TOGETHER THIS BOOK AND FLATTED A LOT OF
THESE COMICS.
THANK YOU TO JORDIE GRALEY FOR TAKING
PHOTOS OF MYSELF, STEF, AND OUR CAT
FAMILY.

THANK YOU TO ALL THE PEOPLE MAKING
COMICS THAT I LOVE. THANK YOU TO
EVERYONE WHO READS MY COMICS,
AND THANK YOU TO EVERYONE WHO
SUPPORTED THE KICKSTARTER
CAMPAIGN FOR THE INITIAL PRINT RUN,
MAKING THIS BOOK A REALITY.

SARAHGRALEY.COM
OURSUPERADVENTURE.COM
@SARAHGRALEYART
FACEBOOK.COM/SARAHGRALEYART
INSTAGRAM.COM/SARAHGRALEY
SONICTHECOMIC.BANDCAMP.COM

SARAHGRALEYART@GMAIL.COM

223

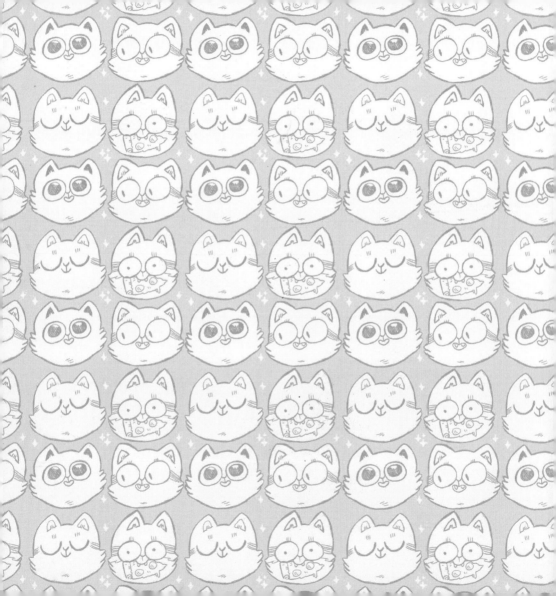